THE SPIRIT OF
TERRORISM

and

REQUIEM FOR THE
TWIN TOWERS

V

Appearing on the first anniversary of the attacks on the World Trade Center and the Pentagon, these three books from Verso present analyses of the United States, the media, and the events surrounding September 11 by Europe's most stimulating and provocative philosophers. Probing beneath the level of TV commentary, political and cultural orthodoxies, and 'rent-a-quote' punditry, Jean Baudrillard, Paul Virilio and Slavoj Žižek offer three highly original and readable accounts that serve as both fascinating introductions to the direction of their respective projects and insightful critiques of the unfolding events. This series seeks to comprehend the philosophical meaning of September 11 and will leave untouched none of the prevailing views currently propagated.

THE SPIRIT OF TERRORISM
Jean Baudrillard

GROUND ZERO
Paul Virilio

WELCOME TO THE DESERT
OF THE REAL!
Slavoj Žižek

THE SPIRIT OF
TERRORISM

and

REQUIEM FOR THE
TWIN TOWERS

———————◆———————

JEAN BAUDRILLARD

Translated by Chris Turner

VERSO
London • New York

This edition first published by Verso 2002
© Verso 2002
Translation © Chris Turner 2002
The Spirit of Terrorism first publised as
L'esprit du terrorisme © Éditions Galilée 2002
Requiem for the Twin Towers first published as
Requiem pour les Twin Towers © Jean Baudrillard 2002

1 3 5 7 9 10 8 6 4 2

Verso
UK: 6 Meard Street, London W1F 0EG
USA: 180 Varick Street, New York, NY 10014–4606
www.versobooks.com

Verso is the imprint of New Left Books

ISBN 1–85984–411–1

British Library Cataloguing in Publication Data
A catalogue record for this book is available from the British Library

Library of Congress Cataloging-in-Publication Data
A catalog record for this book is available from the
Library of Congress

Typeset in Perpetua by M Rules
Printed and bound in the UK by
Biddles Ltd, Guildford and King's Lynn
www.biddles.co.uk

CONTENTS

THE SPIRIT OF
TERRORISM

When it comes to world events, we had seen quite a few. From the death of Diana to the World Cup. And violent, real events, from wars right through to genocides. Yet, when it comes to symbolic events on a world scale – that is to say not just events that gain worldwide coverage, but events that represent a setback for globalization itself – we had had none. Throughout the stagnation of the 1990s, events were 'on strike' (as the Argentinian writer Macedonio Fernandez put it). Well, the strike is over now. Events are not on strike any more. With the attacks on the World

Trade Center in New York, we might even be said to have before us the absolute event, the 'mother' of all events, the pure event uniting within itself all the events that have never taken place.

The whole play of history and power is disrupted by this event, but so, too, are the conditions of analysis. You have to take your time. While events were stagnating, you had to anticipate and move more quickly than they did. But when they speed up this much, you have to move more slowly – though without allowing yourself to be buried beneath a welter of words, or the gathering clouds of war, and preserving intact the unforgettable incandescence of the images.

All that has been said and written is evidence of a gigantic abreaction to the event itself, and the fascination it exerts. The moral condemnation and the holy alliance against terrorism are on the same scale as the prodigious jubilation at seeing this global superpower destroyed – better, at seeing it, in a sense, destroying itself, committing suicide in a blaze of glory. For it is that superpower which, by its unbearable power, has fomented all this violence which is endemic throughout the world, and hence that (unwittingly) terroristic imagination which dwells in all of us.

The fact that we have dreamt of this event, that everyone without exception has dreamt of it — because no one can avoid dreaming of the destruction of any power that has become hegemonic to this degree — is unacceptable to the Western moral conscience. Yet it is a fact, and one which can indeed be measured by the emotive violence of all that has been said and written in the effort to dispel it.

At a pinch, we can say that they *did it*, but we *wished for* it. If this is not taken into account, the event loses any symbolic dimension. It becomes a pure accident, a purely arbitrary act, the murderous phantasmagoria of a few fanatics, and all that would then remain would be to eliminate them. Now, we know very well that this is not how it is.

Which explains all the counterphobic ravings about exorcizing evil: it is because it is there, everywhere, like an obscure object of desire. Without this deep-seated complicity, the event would not have had the resonance it has, and in their symbolic strategy the terrorists doubtless know that they can count on this unavowable complicity.

This goes far beyond hatred for the dominant world power among the disinherited and the exploited, among those who have ended up on the wrong side of the global order. Even those who share in the advantages of that order have this malicious desire in their hearts. Allergy to any definitive order, to any definitive power, is – happily – universal, and the two towers of the World Trade Center were perfect embodiments, in their very twinness, of that definitive order.

No need, then, for a death drive or a destructive instinct, or even for perverse, unintended effects. Very logically – and inexorably – the increase in the power of power heightens the will to destroy it. And it was party to its own destruction. When the two towers collapsed, you had the impression that they were responding to the suicide of the suicide-planes with their own suicides. It has been said that 'Even God cannot declare war on Himself.' Well, He can. The West, in the position of God (divine omnipotence and absolute moral legitimacy), has become suicidal, and declared war on itself.

The countless disaster movies bear witness to this fantasy, which they clearly attempt to exorcize with images, drowning out the whole thing with special effects. But the universal attraction they exert, which is on a par with pornography, shows that acting-out is never very far away, the impulse to reject any system growing all the stronger as it approaches perfection or omnipotence.

It is probable that the terrorists had not foreseen the collapse of the Twin Towers (any more than had the experts!), a collapse which – much more than the attack on the Pentagon – had the greatest symbolic impact. The symbolic collapse of a whole system came about by an unpredictable complicity, as though the towers, by collapsing on their own, by committing suicide, had joined in to round off the event. In a sense, the entire system, by its internal fragility, lent the initial action a helping hand.

The more concentrated the system becomes globally, ultimately forming one single network, the more it becomes vulnerable at a single point (already a single little Filipino hacker had managed, from the dark recesses of his portable computer, to launch the 'I love you' virus, which circled the globe devastating entire networks). Here it was eighteen suicide attackers who, thanks to the absolute weapon of death, enhanced by technological efficiency, unleashed a global catastrophic process.

When global power monopolizes the situation to this extent, when there is such a formidable condensation of all functions in the technocratic machinery, and when no alternative form of thinking is allowed, what other way is there but a *terroristic situational transfer*? It was the system itself which created the objective conditions for this brutal retaliation. By seizing all the cards for itself, it forced the Other to change the rules. And the new rules are fierce ones, because the stakes are fierce. To a system whose very excess of power poses an insoluble challenge, the terrorists respond with a definitive act which is also not susceptible of exchange. Terrorism is the act that restores an irreducible singularity to the heart of a system of generalized exchange. All the singularities (species, individuals and cultures) that have paid with their deaths for the installation of a global circulation governed by a single power are taking their revenge today through this *terroristic situational transfer*.

This is terror against terror – there is no longer any ideology behind it. We are far beyond ideology and politics now. No ideology, no cause – not even the Islamic cause – can account for the energy which fuels terror. The aim is no longer even to transform the world, but (as the heresies did in their day) to radicalize the world by sacrifice. Whereas the system aims to realize it by force.

Terrorism, like viruses, is everywhere. There is a global perfusion of terrorism, which accompanies any system of domination as though it were its shadow, ready to activate itself anywhere, like a double agent. We can no longer draw a demarcation line around it. It is at the very heart of this culture which combats it, and the visible fracture (and the hatred) that pits the exploited and the underdeveloped globally against the Western world secretly connects with the fracture internal to the dominant system. That system can face down any visible antagonism. But against the other kind, which is viral in structure – as though every machinery of domination secreted its own counterapparatus, the agent of its own disappearance – against that form of almost automatic reversion of its own power, the system can do nothing. And terrorism is the shock wave of this silent reversion.

This is not, then, a clash of civilizations or religions, and it reaches far beyond Islam and America, on which efforts are being made to focus the conflict in order to create the delusion of a visible confrontation and a solution based on force. There is, indeed, a fundamental antagonism here, but one which points past the spectre of America (which is, perhaps, the epicentre, but in no sense the sole embodiment, of globalization) and the spectre of Islam (which is not the embodiment of terrorism either), to *triumphant globalization battling against itself*. In this sense, we can indeed speak of a world war – not the Third World War, but the Fourth and the only really global one, since what is at stake is globalization itself. The first two world wars corresponded to the classical image of war. The first ended the supremacy of Europe and the colonial era. The second put an end to Nazism. The third, which has indeed taken place, in the form of cold war and deterrence, put an end to Communism. With each succeeding war, we have moved further towards a single world order. Today that order, which has virtually reached its culmination, finds itself grappling with the antagonistic forces scattered throughout the very heartlands of the global, in all the current convulsions. A fractal war of all cells, all singularities, revolting in the form of antibodies. A confrontation so impossible to pin down that the idea of war has to be rescued from time to time by spectacular set-pieces, such as the Gulf War or the war in Afghanistan. But the Fourth World War is elsewhere. It is what haunts every world order, all hegemonic domination – if Islam dominated the world, terrorism would rise against Islam, *for it is the world, the globe itself, which resists globalization.*

Terrorism is immoral. The World Trade Center event, that symbolic challenge, is immoral, and it is a response to a globalization which is itself immoral. So, let us be immoral; and if we want to have some understanding of all this, let us go and take a little look beyond Good and Evil. When, for once, we have an event that defies not just morality, but any form of interpretation, let us try to approach it with an understanding of Evil.

This is precisely where the crucial point lies – in the total misunderstanding on the part of Western philosophy, on the part of the Enlightenment, of the relation between Good and Evil. We believe naively that the progress of Good, its advance in all fields (the sciences, technology, democracy, human rights), corresponds to a defeat of Evil. No one seems to have understood that Good and Evil advance together, as part of the same movement. The triumph of the one does not eclipse the other – far from it. In metaphysical terms, Evil is regarded as an accidental mishap, but this axiom, from which all the Manichaean forms of the struggle of Good against Evil derive, is illusory. Good does not conquer Evil, nor indeed does the reverse happen: they are at once both irreducible to each other and inextricably interrelated. Ultimately, Good could thwart Evil only by ceasing to be Good since, by seizing for itself a global monopoly of power, it gives rise, by that very act, to a blowback of a proportionate violence.

In the traditional universe, there was still a balance between Good and Evil, in accordance with a dialectical relation which maintained the tension and equilibrium of the moral universe, come what may – not unlike the way the confrontation of the two powers in the Cold War maintained the balance of terror. There was, then, no supremacy of the one over the other. As soon as there was a total extrapolation of Good (hegemony of the positive over any form of negativity, exclusion of death and of any potential adverse force – triumph of the values of Good all along the line), that balance was upset. From this point on, the equilibrium was gone, and it was as though Evil regained an invisible autonomy, henceforward developing exponentially.

Relatively speaking, this is more or less what has happened in the political order with the eclipse of Communism and the global triumph of liberal power: it was at that point that a ghostly enemy emerged, infiltrating itself throughout the whole planet, slipping in everywhere like a virus, welling up from all the interstices of power: Islam. But Islam was merely the moving front along which the antagonism crystallized. The antagonism is everywhere, and in every one of us. So, it is terror against terror. But asymmetric terror. And it is this asymmetry which leaves global omnipotence entirely disarmed. At odds with itself, it can only plunge further into its own logic of relations of force, but it cannot operate on the terrain of the symbolic challenge and death — a thing of which it no longer has any idea, since it has erased it from its own culture.

Up to the present, this integrative power has largely succeeded in absorbing and resolving any crisis, any negativity, creating, as it did so, a situation of the deepest despair (not only for the disinherited, but for the pampered and privileged too, in their radical comfort). The fundamental change now is that the terrorists have ceased to commit suicide for no return; they are now bringing their own deaths to bear in an effective, offensive manner, in the service of an intuitive strategic insight which is quite simply a sense of the immense fragility of the opponent – a sense that a system which has arrived at its quasi-perfection can, by that very token, be ignited by the slightest spark. They have succeeded in turning their own deaths into an absolute weapon against a system that operates on the basis of the exclusion of death, a system whose ideal is an ideal of zero deaths. Every zero-death system is a zero-sum-game system. And all the means of deterrence and destruction can do nothing against an enemy who has already turned his death into a counterstrike weapon. 'What does the American bombing matter? Our men are as eager to die as the Americans are to live!' Hence the non-equivalence of the four thousand deaths inflicted at a stroke on a zero-death system.

Here, then, it is all about death, not only about the violent irruption of death in real time –

'live', so to speak – but the irruption of a death which is far more than real: a death which is symbolic and sacrificial – that is to say, the absolute, irrevocable event.

This is the spirit of terrorism.

Never attack the system in terms of relations of force. That is the (revolutionary) imagination the system itself forces upon you – the system which survives only by constantly drawing those attacking it into fighting on the ground of reality, which is always its own. But shift the struggle into the symbolic sphere, where the rule is that of challenge, reversion and outbidding. *So that death can be met only by equal or greater death.* Defy the system by a gift to which it cannot respond except by its own death and its own collapse.

The terrorist hypothesis is that the system itself will commit suicide in response to the multiple challenges posed by deaths and suicides.

For there is a symbolic obligation upon both the system and power [*le pouvoir*], and in this trap lies the only chance of their catastrophic collapse. In this vertiginous cycle of the impossible exchange of death, the death of the terrorist is an infinitesimal point, but one that creates a gigantic suction or void, an enormous convection. Around this tiny point the whole system of the real and of power [*la puissance*] gathers, transfixed; rallies briefly; then perishes by its own hyperefficiency.

It is the tactic of the terrorist model to bring about an excess of reality, and have the system collapse beneath that excess of reality. The whole derisory nature of the situation, together with the violence mobilized by the system, turns around against it, for terrorist acts are both the exorbitant mirror of its own violence and the model of a symbolic violence forbidden to it, the only violence it cannot exert – that of its own death.

This is why the whole of visible power can do

nothing against the tiny, but symbolic, death of a few individuals.

We have to face facts, and accept that a new terrorism has come into being, a new form of action which plays the game, and lays hold of the rules of the game, solely with the aim of disrupting it. Not only do these people not play fair, since they put their own deaths into play – to which there is no possible response ('they are cowards') – but they have taken over all the weapons of the dominant power. Money and stock-market speculation, computer technology and aeronautics, spectacle and the media networks – they have assimilated everything of modernity and globalism, without changing their goal, which is to destroy that power.

They have even – and this is the height of cunning – used the banality of American everyday life as cover and camouflage. Sleeping in their suburbs, reading and studying with their families, before activating themselves suddenly like time bombs. The faultless mastery of this clandestine style of operation is almost as terroristic as the spectacular act of September 11, since it casts suspicion on any and every individual. Might not any inoffensive person be a potential terrorist? If *they* could pass unnoticed, then each of us is a criminal going unnoticed (every plane also becomes suspect), and in the end, this is no doubt true. This may very well correspond to an unconscious form of potential, veiled, carefully repressed criminality, which is always capable, if not of resurfacing, at least of thrilling secretly to the spectacle of Evil. So the event ramifies down to the smallest detail – the source of an even more subtle mental terrorism.

The radical difference is that the terrorists, while they have at their disposal weapons that are the system's own, possess a further lethal weapon: their own deaths. If they were content just to fight the system with its own weapons, they would immediately be eliminated. If they merely used their own deaths to combat it, they would disappear just as quickly in a useless sacrifice – as terrorism has almost always done up to now (an example being the Palestinian suicide attacks), for which reason it has been doomed to failure.

As soon as they combine all the modern resources available to them with this highly symbolic weapon, everything changes. The destructive potential is multiplied to infinity. It is this multiplication of factors (which seem irreconcilable to us) that gives them such superiority. The 'zero-death' strategy, by contrast, the strategy of the 'clean' technological war, precisely fails to match up to this transfiguration of 'real' power by symbolic power.

The prodigious success of such an attack presents a problem, and if we are to gain some understanding of it, we have to slough off our Western perspective to see what goes on in the terrorists' organization, and in their heads. With us, such efficiency would assume a maximum of calculation and rationality that we find hard to imagine in others. And, even in this case, as in any rational organization or secret service, there would always have been leaks or slip-ups.

So, the secret of such a success lies elsewhere. The difference is that here we are dealing not with an employment contract, but with a pact and a sacrificial obligation. Such an obligation is immune to any defection or corruption. The miracle is to have adapted to the global network and technical protocols, without losing anything of this complicity 'unto death'. Unlike the contract, the pact does not bind individuals – even their 'suicide' is not individual heroism, it is a collective sacrificial act sealed by an ideal demand. And it is the combination of two mechanisms – an operational structure and a symbolic pact – that made an act of such excessiveness possible.

We no longer have any idea what a symbolic calculation is, as in poker or potlatch: with minimum stakes, but the maximum result. And the maximum result was precisely what the terrorists obtained in the Manhattan attack, which might be presented as quite a good illustration of chaos theory: an initial impact causing incalculable consequences; whereas the Americans' massive deployment ('Desert Storm') achieved only derisory effects – the hurricane ending, so to speak, in the beating of a butterfly's wing.

Suicidal terrorism was a terrorism of the poor. This is a terrorism of the rich. This is what particularly frightens us: the fact that they have become rich (they have all the necessary resources) without ceasing to wish to destroy us. Admittedly, in terms of our system of values, they are cheating. It is not playing fair to throw one's own death into the game. But this does not trouble them, and the new rules are not ours to determine.

So any argument is used to discredit their acts. For example, calling them 'suicidal' and 'martyrs' – and adding immediately that martyrdom proves nothing, that it has nothing to do with truth, that it is even (to quote Nietzsche) the enemy number one of truth. Admittedly, their deaths prove nothing, but in a system where truth itself is elusive (or do we claim to possess it?), there is nothing to prove. Moreover, this highly moral argument can be turned around. If the voluntary martyrdom of the suicide bombers proves nothing, then the involuntary martyrdom of the victims of the attack proves nothing either, and there is something unseemly and obscene in making a moral argument out of it (this is in no way to deny their suffering and death).

Another argument in bad faith: these terrorists exchanged their deaths for a place in paradise; their act was not a disinterested one, hence it is not authentic; it would be disinterested only if they did not believe in God, if they saw no hope in death, as is the case with us (yet Christian martyrs assumed precisely such a sublime equivalence). There again, then, they are not fighting fair, since they get salvation, which we cannot even continue to hope for. So we mourn our deaths while they can turn theirs into very high-definition stakes.

Fundamentally, all this – causes, proof, truth, rewards, ends and means – is a typically Western form of calculation. We even evaluate death in terms of interest rates, in value-for-money terms. An economic calculation that is a poor man's calculation – poor men who no longer even have the courage to pay the price.

What can happen now – apart from war, which is itself merely a conventional safety shield [*écran de protection*]? There is talk of bio-terrorism, bacteriological warfare or nuclear terrorism. Yet that is no longer of the order of the symbolic challenge, but of annihilation pure and simple, with no element of risk or glory: it is of the order of the final solution. Now, it is a mistake to see terrorist action as obeying a purely destructive logic. It seems to me that the action of the terrorists, from which death is inseparable (this is precisely what makes it a symbolic act), does not seek the impersonal elimination of the other. Everything lies in the challenge and the duel – that is to say, everything still lies in a dual, personal relation with the opposing power. It is that power which humiliated you, so it too must be humiliated. And not merely exterminated. It has to be made to lose face. And you never achieve that by pure force and eliminating the other party: it must, rather, be targeted and wounded in a genuinely adversarial relation. Apart from the pact that binds the terrorists together, there is also something of a dual pact with the adversary. This is, then, precisely the opposite of the cowardice of which they stand accused, and it is precisely the opposite of what the Americans did in the Gulf War (and which they are currently beginning again in Afghanistan), where the target is invisible and is liquidated operationally.

In all these vicissitudes, what stays with us, above all else, is the sight of the images. This impact of the images, and their fascination, are necessarily what we retain, since images are, whether we like it or not, our primal scene. And, at the same time as they have radicalized the world situation, the events in New York can also be said to have radicalized the relation of the image to reality. Whereas we were dealing before with an uninterrupted profusion of banal images and a seamless flow of sham events, the terrorist act in New York has resuscitated both images and events.

Among the other weapons of the system which they turned round against it, the terrorists exploited the 'real time' of images, their instantaneous worldwide transmission, just as they exploited stock-market speculation, electronic information and air traffic. The role of images is highly ambiguous. For, at the same time as they exalt the event, they also take it hostage. They serve to multiply it to infinity and, at the same time, they are a diversion and a neutralization (this was already the case with the events of 1968). The image consumes the event, in the sense that it absorbs it and offers it for consumption. Admittedly, it gives it unprecedented impact, but impact as image-event.

How do things stand with the real event, then,

if reality is everywhere infiltrated by images, virtuality and fiction? In the present case, we thought we had seen (perhaps with a certain relief) a resurgence of the real, and of the violence of the real, in an allegedly virtual universe. 'There's an end to all your talk about the virtual – this is something real!' Similarly, it was possible to see this as a resurrection of history beyond its proclaimed end. But does reality actually outstrip fiction? If it seems to do so, this is because it has absorbed fiction's energy, and has itself become fiction. We might almost say that reality is jealous of fiction, that the real is jealous of the image. . . . It is a kind of duel between them, a contest to see which can be the most unimaginable.

The collapse of the World Trade Center towers is unimaginable, but that is not enough to make it a real event. An excess of violence is not enough to open on to reality. For reality is a principle, and it is this principle that is lost. Reality and fiction are inextricable, and the fascination with the attack is primarily a fascination with the image (both its exultatory and its catastrophic consequences are themselves largely imaginary).

In this case, then, the real is superadded to the image like a bonus of terror, like an additional *frisson*: not only is it terrifying, but, what is more, it is real. Rather than the violence of the real being there first, and the *frisson* of the image being added to it, the image is there first, and the *frisson* of the real is added. Something like an additional fiction, a fiction surpassing fiction. Ballard (after Borges) talked like this of reinventing the real as the ultimate and most redoubtable fiction.

The terrorist violence here is not, then, a blowback of reality, any more than it is a blowback of history. It is not 'real'. In a sense, it is worse: it is symbolic. Violence in itself may be perfectly banal and inoffensive. Only symbolic violence is generative of singularity. And in this singular event, in this Manhattan disaster movie, the twentieth century's two elements of mass fascination are combined: the white magic of the cinema and the black magic of terrorism; the white light of the image and the black light of terrorism.

We try retrospectively to impose some kind of meaning on it, to find some kind of interpretation. But there is none. And it is the radicality of the spectacle, the brutality of the spectacle, which alone is original and irreducible. The spectacle of terrorism forces the terrorism of spectacle upon us. And, against this immoral fascination (even if it unleashes a universal moral reaction), the political order can do nothing. This is *our* theatre of cruelty, the only one we have left – extraordinary in that it unites the most extreme degree of the spectacular and the highest level of challenge. . . . It is at one and the same time the dazzling micromodel of a kernel of real violence with the maximum possible echo – hence the purest form of spectacle – and a sacrificial model mounting the purest symbolic form of defiance to the historical and political order.

We would forgive them any massacre if it had

a meaning, if it could be interpreted as historical violence – this is the moral axiom of good violence. We would pardon them any violence if it were not given media exposure ('terrorism would be nothing without the media'). But this is all illusion. There is no 'good' use of the media; the media are part of the event, they are part of the terror, and they work in both directions.

The repression of terrorism spirals around as unpredictably as the terrorist act itself. No one knows where it will stop, or what turnabouts there may yet be. There is no possible distinction, at the level of images and information, between the spectacular and the symbolic, no possible distinction between the 'crime' and the crackdown. And it is this uncontrollable unleashing of reversibility that is terrorism's true victory. A victory that is visible in the subterranean ramifications and infiltrations of the event – not just in the direct economic, political, financial slump in the whole of the system – and the resulting moral and psychological downturn –

but in the slump in the value-system, in the whole ideology of freedom, of free circulation, and so on, on which the Western world prided itself, and on which it drew to exert its hold over the rest of the world.

To the point that the idea of freedom, a new and recent idea, is already fading from minds and mores, and liberal globalization is coming about in precisely the opposite form – a police-state globalization, a total control, a terror based on 'law-and-order' measures. Deregulation ends up in a maximum of constraints and restrictions, akin to those of a fundamentalist society.

A fall-off in production, consumption, speculation and growth (but certainly not in corruption!): it is as though the global system were making a strategic fallback, carrying out a painful revision of its values – in defensive reaction, as it would seem, to the impact of terrorism, but responding, deep down, to its secret injunctions: enforced regulation as a product of absolute disorder, but a regulation it imposes on itself – internalizing, as it were, its own defeat.

Another aspect of the terrorists' victory is that all other forms of violence and the destabilization of order work in its favour. Internet terrorism, biological terrorism, the terrorism of anthrax and rumour – all are ascribed to Bin Laden. He might even claim natural catastrophes as his own. All the forms of disorganization and perverse circulation operate to his advantage. The very structure of generalized world trade works in favour of impossible exchange. It is like an 'automatic writing' of terrorism, constantly refuelled by the involuntary terrorism of news and information. With all the panic consequences which ensue; if, in the current anthrax scare,* the hysteria spreads spontaneously by instantaneous crystallization, like a chemical solution at the mere contact of a molecule, this is because the whole system has reached a critical mass which makes it vulnerable to any aggression.

* This text was written in October 2001 and published in *Le Monde* on November 3 2001.

There is no remedy for this extreme situation, and war is certainly not a solution, since it merely offers a rehash of the past, with the same deluge of military forces, bogus information, senseless bombardment, emotive and deceitful language, technological deployment and brainwashing. Like the Gulf War: a non-event, an event that does not really take place.

And this indeed is its *raison-d'être*: to substitute, for a real and formidable, unique and unforeseeable event, a repetitive, rehashed pseudo-event. The terrorist attack corresponded to a precedence of the event over all interpretative models; whereas this mindlessly military, technological war corresponds, conversely, to the model's precedence over the event, and hence to a conflict over phoney stakes, to a situation of 'no contest'. War as continuation of the absence of politics by other means.

REQUIEM FOR THE
TWIN TOWERS

A version of this paper was Baudrillard's contribution to a debate on the events of September 11 2001, the 'Rencontres philosophiques outre-Atlantique', organized jointly by New York University and France Culture in Washington Square, Manhattan. The formal contributions were broadcast on France Culture on the afternoon of February 23 2002. The debate, which was largely conducted in French, was chaired by Tom Bishop; other participants were Jacques Rancière, Charles Larmore and Mark Lilla. The footnotes, which refer to slight variations between the written text and the version delivered in New York, are my own [Trans.].

The September 11 attacks also concern architecture, since what was destroyed was one of the
most prestigious of buildings, together with a
whole (Western) value-system and a world order.[1]

1   In the New York debate, Baudrillard prefaced his talk
    with the following comments: 'There is an absolute dif-
    ficulty in speaking of an absolute event. That is to say, in
    providing an analysis of it that is not an explanation – as
    I don't think there is any possible explanation of
    this event, either by intellectuals or by others – but its
    analogon, so to speak; an analysis which might possibly
    be as unacceptable as the event, but strikes the . . . let
    us say, symbolic imagination in more or less the same
    way.'

It may, then, be useful to begin with a historical and architectural analysis of the Twin Towers, in order to grasp the symbolic significance of their destruction.

First of all, why the *Twin* Towers? Why *two* towers at the World Trade Center?

All Manhattan's tall buildings had been content to confront each other in a competitive verticality, and the product of this was an architectural panorama reflecting the capitalist system itself – a pyramidal jungle, whose famous image stretched out before you as you arrived from the sea. That image changed after 1973, with the building of the World Trade Center. The effigy of the system was no longer the obelisk and the pyramid, but the punch card and the statistical graph. This architectural graphism is the embodiment of a system that is no longer competitive, but digital and countable, and from which competition has disappeared in favour of networks and monopoly.

Perfect parallelepipeds, standing over 1,300 feet tall, on a square base. Perfectly balanced, blind communicating vessels (they say terrorism is 'blind', but the towers were blind too – monoliths no longer opening on to the outside world, but subject to artificial conditioning[2]). The fact that there were two of them signifies the end of any original reference. If there had been only one, monopoly would not have been perfectly embodied. Only the doubling of the sign truly puts an end to what it designates.

There is a particular fascination in this reduplication. However tall they may have been, the

---

2   In New York, Baudrillard here glossed: 'Air condition-ing, but mental conditioning too'.

two towers signified, none the less, a halt to verticality. They were not of the same breed as the other buildings. They culminated in the exact reflection of each other. The glass and steel façades of the Rockefeller Center buildings still mirrored each other in an endless specularity. But the Twin Towers no longer had any façades, any faces. With the rhetoric of verticality disappears also the rhetoric of the mirror. There remains only a kind of black box, a series closed on the figure two, as though architecture, like the system, was now merely a product of cloning, and of a changeless genetic code.

New York is the only city in the world that has, throughout its history, tracked the present form of the system and all its many developments with such prodigious fidelity. We must, then, assume that the collapse of the towers – itself a unique event in the history of modern cities – prefigures a kind of dramatic ending and, all in all,

44

disappearance both of this form of architecture and of the world system it embodies. Shaped in the pure computer image of banking and finance, (ac)countable and digital, they were in a sense its brain, and in striking there the terrorists have struck at the brain, at the nerve-centre of the system.

The violence of globalization also involves architecture, and hence the violent protest against it also involves the destruction of that architecture. In terms of collective drama, we can say that the horror for the 4,000 victims of dying in those towers was inseparable from the horror of living in them – the horror of living and working in sarcophagi of concrete and steel.

These architectural monsters, like the Beaubourg Centre, have always exerted an ambiguous fascination, as have the extreme forms of modern technology in general – a contradictory feeling

of attraction and repulsion, and hence, somewhere, a secret desire to see them disappear. In the
case of the Twin Towers, something particular is
added: precisely their symmetry and their
twin-ness. There is, admittedly, in this cloning and
perfect symmetry an aesthetic quality, a kind of
perfect crime against form, a tautology of form
which can give rise, in a violent reaction, to the
temptation to break that symmetry, to restore an
asymmetry, and hence a singularity.

Their destruction itself respected the symmetry of the towers: a double attack, separated by a
few minutes' interval, with a sense of suspense
between the two impacts. After the first, one
could still believe it was an accident. Only the second impact confirmed the terrorist attack. And in
the Queens air crash a month later, the TV sta-
tions waited, staying with the story (in France) for
four hours, waiting to broadcast a possible second
crash 'live'. Since that did not occur, we shall

never know now whether it was an accident or a terrorist act.

The collapse of the towers is the major symbolic event. Imagine they had not collapsed, or only one had collapsed: the effect would not have been the same at all. The fragility of global power would not have been so strikingly proven. The towers, which were the emblem of that power, still embody it in their dramatic end, which resembles a suicide. Seeing them collapse themselves, as if by implosion, one had the impression that they were committing suicide in response to the suicide of the suicide planes.

Were the Twin Towers destroyed, or did they collapse? Let us be clear about this: the two towers are both a physical, architectural object and a symbolic object[3] (symbolic of financial power and

3 In New York, Baudrillard added: 'symbolic in the weak sense, but symbolic, for all that'.

global economic liberalism). The architectural object was destroyed, but it was the symbolic object which was targeted and which it was intended to demolish. One might think the physical destruction brought about the symbolic collapse. But in fact no one, not even the terrorists, had reckoned on the total destruction of the towers. It was, in fact, their symbolic collapse that brought about their physical collapse, not the other way around.

As if the power bearing these towers suddenly lost all energy, all resilience; as though that arrogant power suddenly gave way under the pressure of too intense an effort: the effort always to be the unique world model.

So the towers, tired of being a symbol which was too heavy a burden to bear, collapsed, this time physically, in their totality. Their nerves of steel cracked. They collapsed vertically, drained of their strength, with the whole world looking on in astonishment.

The symbolic collapse came about, then, by a kind of unpredictable complicity – as though the entire system, by its internal fragility, joined in the game of its own liquidation, and hence joined in the game of terrorism. Very logically, and inexorably, the increase in the power of power heightens the will to destroy it. But there is more: somewhere, it was party to its own destruction. The countless disaster movies bear witness to this fantasy, which they attempt to exorcize with images and special effects. But the fascination they exert is a sign that acting-out is never very far away – the rejection of any system, including internal rejection, growing all the stronger as it approaches perfection or omnipotence. It has been said that 'Even God cannot declare war on Himself.' Well, He can. The West, in the position of God (divine omnipotence and absolute moral legitimacy), has become suicidal, and declared war on itself.

Even in their failure, the terrorists succeeded beyond their wildest hopes: in bungling their attack on the White House (while succeeding far beyond their objectives on the towers), they demonstrated unintentionally that that was not the essential target, that political power no longer means much, and real power lies else-where. As for what should be built in place of the towers, the problem is insoluble. Quite sim-ply because one can imagine nothing equivalent that would be worth destroying – that would be worthy of being destroyed. The Twin Towers were worth destroying. One cannot say the same of many architectural works. Most things are not even worth destroying or sacrificing. Only works of prestige deserve that fate, for it is an honour. This proposition is not as paradoxical as it sounds, and it raises a basic issue for architecture: one should build only those things which, by their excellence, are worthy of being destroyed. Take a look around with this radical proposition in mind, and you will see what a pass we have come to. Not much would withstand this extreme hypothesis.

This brings us back to what should be the basic question for architecture, which architects never formulate: is it normal to build and construct? In fact it is not, and we should preserve the absolutely problematical character of the undertaking. Undoubtedly, the task of architecture – of good architecture – is to efface itself, to disappear as such. The towers, for their part, have disappeared. But they have left us the symbol of their disappearance, their disappearance as symbol. They, which were the symbol of omnipotence, have become, by their absence, the symbol of the possible disappearance of that omnipotence – which is perhaps an even more potent symbol.

Whatever becomes of that global omnipotence, it will have been destroyed here for a moment.

Moreover, although the two towers have disappeared, they have not been annihilated. Even in their pulverized state, they have left behind an intense awareness of their presence. No one who knew them can cease imagining them and the imprint they made on the skyline from all points of the city. Their end in material space has borne them off into a definitive imaginary space. By the grace of terrorism, the World Trade Center has become the world's most beautiful building – the eighth wonder of the world![4]

4   After delivering a slightly modified version of this last paragraph in New York, Baudrillard closed with the comment: 'So I set out to produce a Requiem, but it was also, in a way, a Te Deum.'